MW01129809

Spark

A BOOK ABOUT THOUGHT

Dedicated to my husband, Yanky. I'm honored and blessed to share this journey with you. This book would not have happened without you.

Thank you Rivkah, Matthue, and DLR for your help with this book.

FIRST EDITION: FEBRUARY 2017

Second Printing: October 2018

© 2016 by Esty Raskin • All Rights Reserved

ISBN: 978-0-9984041-2-7

LCCN: 2016920062

Inside>Out Press
Brooklyn, NY
718-913-7800

This is Spark.

This is where Spark comes from.

I think it's called...sparkness.

Spark likes to talk.

A lot.

Spark can talk so much that he gets **buried** under his words!

But you know
he's there, because
someone's gotta be
making all that noise!

Spark can make
everything look
wonderful...

Or he can make you
feel miserable.

That's just how he is.

He is **always** coming up with something to say.

In your head!

That is, if he's **your** Spark.
My Spark likes to hang out in **my** head.

He chatters in there all day long!

Sometimes, he repeats the same thing over and over.

If you forget that he's there, he will just keep on going...

But if you say, "Hi, Spark!"...

He might
start to tell
you
something
new.

FOR PARENTS AND EDUCATORS: WHAT IS THOUGHT?

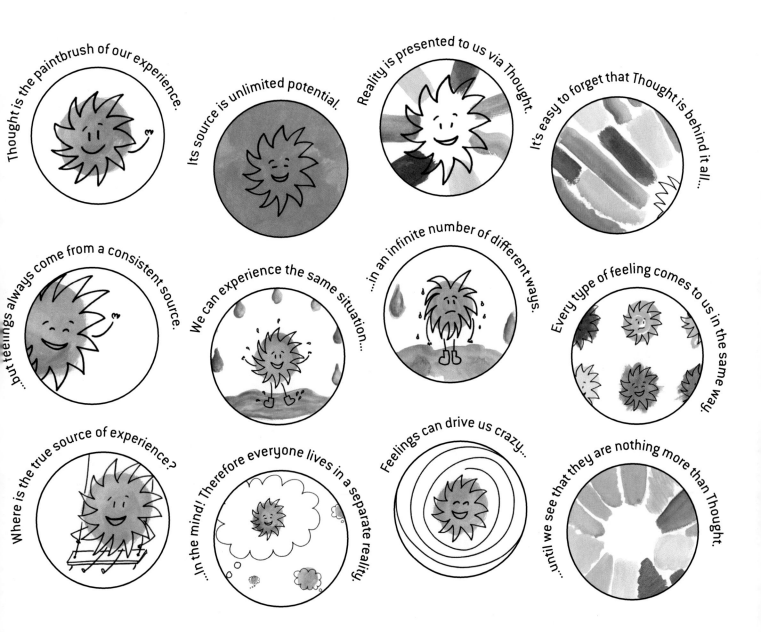

Thought is the paintbrush of our experience.

Its source is unlimited potential.

Reality is presented to us via Thought.

It's easy to forget that Thought is behind it all...

...but feelings always come from a consistent source.

We can experience the same situation...

...in an infinite number of different ways.

Every type of feeling comes to us in the same way.

Where is the true source of experience?

...In the mind! Therefore everyone lives in a separate reality.

Feelings can drive us crazy...

...until we see that they are nothing more than Thought.

What types of thinking are you feeling today?

Made in the USA
Las Vegas, NV
30 January 2025

17203403R00019